Full Frontal Tenudity

Published in the USA by:
BearManor Media
PO Box 1129
Duncan, Oklahoma 73534-1129
www.bearmanormedia.com

ISBN 978-1-59393-587-0 (Hardcover)
ISBN 978-1-59393-586-3 (Paperback)

Printed in the United States of America.

Full Frontal Tenudity

..*And stoner snacks for Love Slaves!*

By JUDY TENUTA

Listen, Little Marshmallows of Mirth— the way to a man's heart is through his pants, but if you want to keep that hulk of walking, squawking ATM, you'll have to feed him… And not just his ego, although it always helps to reinforce the belief that he has a rocket booster in his pants. But besides building his self esteem, you must be able to whip up really great munchies especially during football season. And one doesn't have to smoke like a stoner to eat like one. The goddess certainly approves of all hemp heads who must partake of the pipe to survive. Unfortunately the goddess must be coherent & not stare at light fixtures in between vodka shots at performing arts centers.

This book is a collection of recipes for food, friends and fun! A kind of "chicken soup for your crotch", if you will. Yes it's warm and fuzzy and makes you want to plots like your Nana watching the wheel of fortune while slurping a bowl of borscht. In this book I will divulge my deepest secrets, helpful tips, and poignant stories that will help make you an holistically hot hostess. You will be transformed from your pupa/larva stage of loneliness, into a great goddess gourmet of ganja. You will spread your wings and be a knoshing nymph, not just in the kitchen, but in every room of your trailer, and sometimes even in a Walmart produce section (the greatest love of all).

Join me on a journey into another world. Follow me into the light of your future. A light that will help guide you through the endless chain of "man pigs". A light that might turn out to be a police flashlight shined into your eyes at four am while you're car radio blasts Lynyrd Skynyrd.

This book will change your life and the lives of your family that you haven't seen or spoken to since the boxer rebellion

…It could happen!

I would like to spank, I mean thank...

LANCE PERKINS
Art direction and editing

JAMES FRANKLIN
For his fantasmic photos and front cover design

DAVE SHELTON
For his great cartoon drawings of my jokes

GARY GLADSTONE
All the fun photos of The Goddess and friends

ALAN MERCER
For his lovely shots of The Goddess

My Many Photo Posers:
***Downtown Julie Brown, Cher Rue,
Scott Silverman, Richard Sebastian***
All the hot models and actors from my video stills.

Special thanks to my Brother **Dan Bosco**, *who grew up with me eating like a stoner, and told me to write a stoner snack book which has evolved into* **3 MINI BOOKS IN ONE:**

I. JUDY'S HOLLYWOOD TO ENGLISH DICTIONARY
2. JUDY'S SASSY STONER SNACKS
3 . 40 WAYS TO BREED A LOVE SLAVE

JUDY'S "HOLLYWOOD TO ENGLISH DICTIONARY"

Dear Love-Slaves, in Hollywood, no one ever says what they really mean, so I have broken down some frequently used phrases, so you know what the BITCHES REALLY MEAN!

NOW SNUGGLE UP WITH A SASSY STONER SNACK (and/or love-tart) AND LETS GET STARTED!

Great to see you again =
Who the hell are you?

We're going another way for your part =
We're casting Lindsay Lohan as you!

Best friends forever =
We wave to each other on the red carpet

I Love your hair =
Your weave sucks, BEE-OTCH!

We'll talk later =
Get the f--k away from me!

Let's do lunch =
Good luck getting a hold of me!

I'm always on time =
I'll be 40 min.. late

I know your ex-husband =
We bonked at your wedding

I'm in a pilot =
I'm a male flight attendant

Let's meet at your place =
I live with my mother

I have a 3 picture deal =
I live in a shopping cart

I made a ton of money last year =
I'm filing for bankruptcy

My friends say I look just like you =
I'm a 2'1" Guidette

I'm friends with all my exes =
I only date plastic surgeons

I'm under 40 =
Hurray for Photoshop!

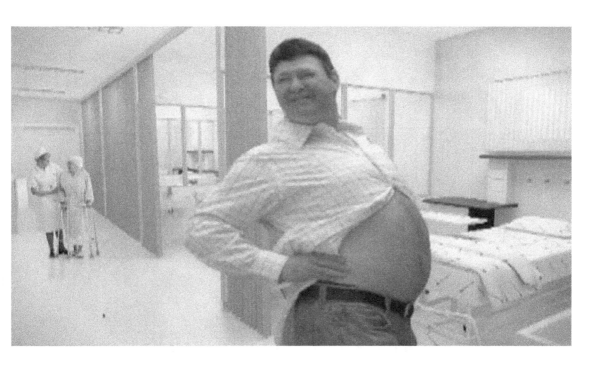

I'm medium build =
I have a giant beer gut

I only drink to unwind =
I'm married to Jack Daniels

I'm a successful screenwriter =
I'm in AA

I'll make it worth your while =
I'm a big, fat HO!

Your business card will come in handy =
I'm out of toilet paper

Beverly Hills Housewife! = Fish lip alert!

I have 6,000 friends all over the world =
I'm addicted to Facebook

I can dance in these 8 " heels =
I'm a Drag Queen

I just got out of jail =
I just posed nude for Playboy

I can't do long distance relationships =
YOUR DICK ISN'T LONG ENOUGH

I'm so busy, I forget to eat =
I'm a coked up super model

Do me a favor? =
Buy me some tampons

I used to be a size 0 =
I have to buy 2 seats in coach

His divorce is almost final =
He's married & broke

I have to hurry to my photo shoot =
The Botox is wearing off

I'll call you back, I'm in a meeting =
I'm having sex with your wife

Please let's be friends =
I'm going to f--k you without having sex

I'm a great intern =
I swallowed the leader

Do you have any crystal meth? =
I'm a soccer mom

He cleans my pool =
he's great in bed

My gardener just saw me naked =
What was he doing at target

Wanna meet the twins? =
Check my new implants

Who needs talent to be on TV =
Meet the Lardashians

I finally married my soulmate =
He's a billionaire on a respirator

I'm a congressman =
I'm gonna sext you my wiener

My wife & I need a maid = I'm the
Sperminator, let me puff you up!

My plate is really full right now =
Buzz off, Bozo!

I'm up till 5am =
I'm a flippin vampire!

You have a great smile =
Your lip gloss is blinding

I don't eat animals =
I just ride them!

Wow what an ass! You're either a lawyer or Kim Kardashian

I live at the gym and never do carbs =
HELLO, I'm a gay man

I'm losing my short term memory =
What did I just say?

Lets have a Jewish Christmas =
Let's do Chinese and a movie!

I love the outdoors =
I sell oranges on the freeway

I want a strong career woman =
Support my unemployed ass

Lets honeymoon in Aruba =
I have a million dollar policy on you...

I love your work =
I just saw your sex tape!

Your sister is hot!! =
We're in west Hollywood, this is my dad!

I'm psychic =
I'm psychotic

Marry me now =
I need a green card

There's someone for everyone =
just don't deflate her!

When is it due?... Uh oh. =
You've been living at Hometown Buffet

I just got arrested =
I'm an A-Lister at last

I'm a big Hollywood producer =
Get a shovel for this conversation

You're too young for this role =
Words you'll never hear in Hollywood"

I'm a serious actor =
I just got out of Betty Ford!

Our breakup was mutual =
She caught me cheating

I'll splurge & buy you coffee =
I have a net worth of $6.

I'm a transgender librarian = I can sing the whole score from "CATS"

The History of Judy

The Goddess started playing "Man's Country"…a gay bathhouse, in the mid eighties. I felt like the Bette Milder of Chicago. Ooooooh, let's go back in time; I'll never forget I was asked to perform for the steamy towel boys on Halloween of 1985. At that time I was but a delicate flower in my late twenties, (it could happen, pigs! Anyway, my parents begged to come with me, to which I replied, "mom, dad, I don't think you're ready for this jelly!" Because they are soooooooooo Catholic, but at the same time, kind of hip. (After all I am their daughter). So I'm performing in my prom gown, and my parents are sitting off to the side as the hot boys in towels are rolling all over each other, and afterward, my mom says" oh Honey, that was so sweet the way your jokes made those boys want to kiss and hug on the floor." And I didn't want to burst her bubble, so I said, "Yeah, mom. I guess I'm like the Barry White of comedy to them. And my dad said," well there should be more love like that in the world." So like the Petite Flower, Giver-Goddess, my parents were also routing for the gays. I just wish I knew which jokes made them want to ravage each other. Maybe it was, "how many of you ever started dating some pig, cuz you were too lazy to commit suicide". That gets most virgins moist.

I especially remember spring of 1996. International Mr. Leather, they picked me up in a stretch limo, with my mom, brothers & former love pig, it was at the Old Chicago Theater. The leather studs were tonguing in the prime seats and 2 guys with their chaps down, and my mom scolds, "cant you wait until my daughter is off stage to mount each other?" Then in the middle of my act, this anorexic queen in head to toe tattoos jumps onstage to lick my boots while I'm singing the Pope song on my squeezebox. It could happen!

Accessories

It's just offensive that Octomom & Kate took a tub of fertility drugs, popped out a soccer team, and then had to subject us to their daily scream fest on a reality show. Paris Hilton made chijuajua an accessory, but now that she's not in prison for blonde possession & has devoted herself to charity (free sex to shipping magnates), doggie satchels have become passé. Now babies in birkins have boomed on the red carpet.. Now babies are even popping out babies, and bragging about it on "teen mom"! This is how America gets back to work: rewarding single knocked up teens with TV shows. In this economy, I need a Chinese baby to adopt me. It is my dream to one day open a daycare center… of 28 yr. old boys. It could happen!

All of young and not so young Hollywood is puffin up and popping out kids. Why? Because kids are the new accessory. You see moms at the mall with kids no longer on leashes, but bouncing in their designer bags! It's not so bad when Brangelina & Spice Girl Beckham wear kids like purses, because at least they can afford a goo-goo Gucci baby. And then Madonna copycats Brangelina & buys a couple of kids from Africa. These are the luckiest accessories.

Hot For Homeless Hoarders

Like I've said to all of my B.F.F.'s who whine that " I can't find a good man"- hey stop dating hoarders are hot- you can fill trash bags full of their crap & give it to the homeless. Do not trust a man with a beard unless he's riding a sleigh full of reindeer. Guys just because you've got face hair, it doesn't mean you're a magician, OK? It's going to take more than a quarter to appear from behind your ear to saw me in half with your sex sword. I used to think guys with beards were mysterious I- no they're just too damn lazy to shave…hey if every Halloween I have to trick or treat for some candy apples to shave my legs, then, you can Supercut that rat's nest round your jaw.

My Big Fat Secret

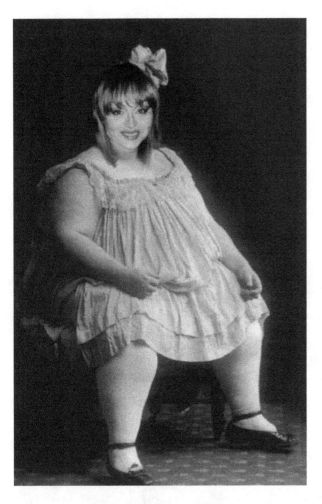

I've destroyed all childhood photos from ages 14 to 16, when I ballooned into a planet in high school. I was so fat I couldn't walk, I just rolled around like a giant blimp, and in those days, you couldn't go on a reality show with personal trainers to whip you into shape. Just join Weight Watchers- I would only eat tuna minus Mayo for 2 days & I was barfing like a 200 lb. supermodel. I was soooo fat, my moons would collide and I just couldn't control myself around food, especially French donuts and pizza. For breakfast, I'd inhale a dozen eggs, on whole-wheat toast, so at least I was a healthy minded heifer... I was so embarrassed about my girth that in high school, I would hide in the girls' restroom and wolf down an apple and Cheetos, so classmates wouldn't make fun of me in the lunchroom. I mean, I was bigger than a French brothel on fat Tuesday! As a senior in high school, I rolled into prom and while dancing with abandon to "I'm too sexy " and popped a baby out on the floor. I was soo fat I didn't even know I was pregnant. I know every non-fat person says, "How could you not know you were pregnant? You just keep filling a void of loneliness with Twinkies and tacos, you don't look in the mirror, obviously not paying attention to your health, so you don't even notice your period has stopped. I was just as classless as all the trailer trash teen moms on vh1, but at least I had the good sense to realize that as an immature 17 yr.. old, who couldn't even take care of myself & my eating habits, the best choice for my pretend baby was to tell my Mom she had an "hysterical pregnancy", thus the "Petite Flower" was born.

Sassy in Seattle

One of the most outrageous moments onstage was at a Seattle comedy club in 1995. I was pontificating about "Goddessness", something to the effect, "you know what happens when you fall in love…you lose control of your reasoning powers"…and as I'm saying this, a beautiful blonde girl around the age of 25 walks right up to the stage and kisses me smack on the mouth- I don't know what shocked me more…a kiss from a girl in the middle of my act, or that there could be an attractive girl in Seattle (oh Geisha why you talk so bad?).

Get Out Of The Closet And Into Your Life

Who would think that in the year 2011 after the success of queer as folk, there are still closeted gay married men. I mean even the Nazi pope comes out on the balcony in his Vera Wang white wedding smock!! So get out of your screams and into your gay lifestyle! Like hello, the former governor McGreedy of New Jersey, who's poor wife had no clue her husband was gay, except for the fact that he'd sniff poppers & go clubbing every night till 4am-take a cat nap till noon then do brunch with his "staff: interior designer, hair dresser, & pool boy, Eduardo. Plus, every time the Gov. & wifey had sex, he'd make her wear a Jake Gylenhall mask while playing the soundtrack from "Liza with a Z". How gay is that?

Let that be a warning to women who are questioning what team their husband is really on. Here's the undercover gay test: If hubby starts tapping his feet and whipping his head back while listening to Cher's "Believe", then starts weeping uncontrollably during " Judy Garland's "Live at Carnegie Hall" that's a giant tip off he's begging to be a bottom. In my own life, I was first married to a guy everyone thought was gay but wasn't… he was just weird. Then I lived with a guy whom everyone but me thought was gay, but he was super closeted. How did I finally figure this out after 10 years of living with La Cage a fool? He would always profess to hate Streisand, but after I was forced to kick him out for peeing some other girl's name in the snow, I checked his iPod and he had 6 different rage mixes of "Papa Can You Hear Me"...Get a clue. Jude. Hmmmm…no wonder he only wanted to have sex from behind. He'd pull my hair and shout, "hey Jude, hey Jude"! For a split second, I thought he was Paul McCartney. (Right like he's worthy to lick Paul McCartney's G-string (on his guitar, gutter-hogs!)

So many petite flowers, including myself, are drawn to quiet, sensitive men. (Code 4 undercover gay). I would be willing to bet that at least 50 percent of women have loved, lived with and even popped out children by undercover gays. Take for example Gynormica= a full figured singer who performed at every gay event in West Hollyweird. For the past 20 years. She looked like Ursula the undersea witch from the little mermaid, except not as cute. Yes, that was nasty, but you live for it! Anyway her flaming "husband", brad was also her manager. Every time he opened his mouth, gay dachshunds within a ten-mile radius would start howling. I would say to our mutual friends, "do you think Gynormica knows Brad is gay? & She's hoping to convert him?"

And they'd say, "They both secretly know it but don't dare mention the ginormous pink elephant in the room because it works for them? She's a big fag hag who adores the attention of gay men ...So she might as well be married to one. And he has to keep up the appearance of being straight until his super catholic mother croaks.

I myself am like a gay man in drag but without the drama…. Not!! Lots of drama! My gay men keep me thin. They workout all morning, then don't eat carbs. These hot queens slap the croissant out of my hands – "Girl- do you want your thighs to turn into redwoods- step away from the carbs!! Every time you walk those tree trunks will start a fire. Do you want to be responsible for torching Tarzana? Yeah!

Then there's the troll who side=swipes my Mercedes as he's speeding through the alley like a bat out of hell. As I scream, "look what you just did to my car", he retorts, "Judy, don't you remember me, we had lunch @ pink taco 3 years ago…. I scream, "focus, bitch, you just scraped my Lexus with your stupid ford focus side view mirror. He's like, "but don't you remember? We met on match and had lunch at the galleria. "I'm like, "dude, you have black toenails and you're wearing flip-flops, there's no way I'd spit my gum in your direction. What are you gonna do to fix my car? He's like you can buff it out with mind control".. This jackal lope needed a reverse circumcision.. He suggests we go next door to the car wash to get it buffed out. Rodrigo, the buffer says "No way, you have to take this to car to your dealer for a major facelift." To which black toenails retorts, "Can't I just take you to lunch?" Yeah like a soup and spamwich special at Arby's makes up for $2,000 dent…not! Lesson: just because a pig runs into you, doesn't mean you should share his hotpocket…nasty!

Friends Are Just Enemies Who Don't Have The Guts To Kill You.

The way to a love hog's heart is through his pants, preferably with a lap dance. But first seduce the sex donkey through his stomach. So many sub virgins complain to the goddess about lack of attention from her man, once he has the remote, in fact here is a letter: "Dear Goddess, how can I get my guy to pay attention to me during football, baseball & basketball games?"

Little virtual vixens, what do you think halftime is for? Teasing the pig with sassy snacks…. That's what! ****Major league footnote for getting your pigs attention during the NFL playoffs. Learn from my personal experience…and here it is: I can't believe this just happened to The Goddess: the Cowboys just got crushed by the Vikings & my love pig who is almost always ready to switch from couch potato to pokey-man, just sits there as I plop on his lap in my hot zebra print mini dress with my boobs popping out & and says, shouldn't you be writing your book? Which is code for:" he didn't take his little blue pill, so he couldn't get it up even if Megan Fox Pole danced on his piccolo…Okay, maybe Megan Fox, but definitely not Renee Zellweger. No offense, but how does that squint-bucket get cast as the object of men's desire in so many great films like Leatherheads &? She looks like an underfed catcher's mit sucking on a lemon, and I have yet to see her eyes…does she have any? We need to resurrect Leonard Nimoy "in search of Zellweger's orbs. I mean it as a friend.

Now to return to the original subject: male attention, I'm really glad that my suppressed sex slug didn't take his blue pill, cuz now I'm writing like a semi-non prolific Joyce Carol Oates with a sense of humor, while he's watching the jets get butt-slammed by the chargers…so I'll get published while he's retaining beer for the Superbowl! But strangely enough, I get much more work done when he's in the next room getting brain drained by ESPN. And this brings me to my next point about relationships. They're not just about sex, they're about having a breathing body in the next room to scream at when the toilet overflows, or the roof caves in from the earthquake. Mostly I need a guy with a samurai sword to bust open the impenetrable plastic packaging on my Venus leg razors, triple AAA batteries, and all objects sold at CVS…not even my ginsu knives can cut through that crap. I was recently sent a nativity scene hermetically sealed in super ballistic plastic, and while slashing it open, the 3 Kings got maimed into looking like the 3 Stooges in swaddling clothes.

Stoner's Snack Attack

Attention all Stoners & non Stoners who snack like Stoners:
First of all, I work with many Stoners. Because, by definition, comedians & musicians are Stoners, so even though I don't doobie, because it spaces me out to the point where George W. possesses me. And can't complete a sentence, I certainly appreciate other artists who get their creative groove jamming with the jamba.

Also we all know that Stoners are too baked to cook- and when you can't even throw it together with a few pals in the kitchen you might have to roll over to iHop- where you come hungry & leave hefty. Just order a stack of pancakes topped with potato chips, & smothered in a ton of butter and maple syrup. Yumm make sure you laugh hysterically at the waitress from hell between bites so you can burn up all these gazillions of fat calories!

For a quick munchie fix at home. Mix a ½ box of powdered sugar,
1/4 Stick of butter 1 teaspoon of vanilla extract, 4-5 tablespoons of extra crunchy peanut butter and spread on apple slices and or your favorite finger & enjoy while watching fat chicks on QVC sell skinny jeans.

Here are some recipes to reactivate your sports obsessed studcicle during his ESPN trance. The goddess will now dispel the myth that you have to eat rabbit food to lose weight! Nooooo, do not deprive yourself …do not inhale the whole mud pie; just have 3 big beasty bites or 5 petite bites. As a sidebar, The Goddess can't spend hours cooking, which is why stoner recipes are perfect: they are both tasty and time efficient.

For the trailer trash man-boy: don your daisy duke short shorts, do the 2 step while making him eat Spam"n eggs off your legs, just like a younger, hotter Martha Stewart in prison with a sassy cellmate like Rachel Ray…ok that would make you a nearly coherent Jessica Simpson. Then shout a cheer like a Laker girl: we're having spam & eggs, it tastes so good on my legs, spam and eggs are really neat! Spam & eggs are fun 2 eat! Spam & eggs just can't be beat! … Hooray!! For Spam & eggs!!"

Invite your drunk yoga instructor girlfriend over to your condo & lick Nutella off her tummy while your man hog is tied to the bed screaming for the video camera remember boys and girls, pink tacos are fat free!! FYI; yoga instructors are major potheads; they have to be high to twist themselves into those crazy pretzel positions. My good friend Brendy was a yogi and when she wasn't twisted into a doggie circus balloon she was on the bong. I wouldn't be surprised if Miley Cyrus is a yogi she's bongin out with her BFF's, by the time she's 19 she'll sound like Linda Blair in the exorcist ...oh wait, she already does!

Lay down on the coffee table in front of your couch potato, roll a cheese ball all over your body while he scrapes it off with low fat wheat thins like the Keebler elf devilishly dipping his crackers into the cheese ball your aunt Margie sent for Christmas! The hated cheese ball that was kicked around like a soccer ball is suddenly savory!

When you combine TV snacks with foreplay, you get a double dose of pleasure: for your tummy and woo- woo! For dessert, dip your toes in the chocolate fountain he gave you 4 Valentine's Day and make him lick those tootsies clean. This is a perfect stay at home activity for a rainy day. Especially after big romantic holidays like ground hog's day

  To fight man-child obesity, wrap a powdered donut in fried bologna, serve with a side of pork-in-beans on his Gameboy!

  Or deep-fried bowtie pasta smothered in cheese whiz and dipped in hot marinara sauce.

  No time to microwave? Cold Spaghetti-oos and milk during the Simpsons. For dessert: deep-fried gummy worms wrapped in bacon, shoved inside a glazed donut hole.

Lets not forget our four legged friends: chef Boy-R-Dee spaghetti & meatballs shared with your shiatsu during Animal Planet's Doggie Whisperer.

There's nothing hotter on a summer's day than two buffed up twinkies covered in hot fudge, whipped crème, nuts and a cherry… just kiss and serve! But only after these hot Adonis twins have rubbed & buffed you in the hot tub.

Devour grilled cheese & root beer float after jumping through hoops, screaming at automated Bank of America phone whore to make a withdrawal.

Booze & implants- you need plenty of both if you're gonna be one of the sluts next door on hef's lap at the Playboy mansion.

Balloon Boy in a meat coat smothered in BBQ sauce during 4th of July cookout. Even Lady Gaga would plop herself on the grill in her prom gown made of meat!

Indulge in guacamoli & chips with a side of mac & cheese while Bill O'Reilly uses Ann Coulter to mix his martini while covering the Republican National Convention. Glenn Beck on a stick, with Pirate's Booty & Heineken chaser. Glenn Beck on any sharp object would be a must have for any Democratic get together.

Ben and Jerry's chunkie monkey and Ruffles potato chips, after a breakup with your cheating pig.

Indulge in red velvet cupcakes with cream cheese frosting and walnuts with cold milk. And for dessert: tortilla chips dipped in german chocolate cake & vanilla ice-cream in celebration of a super sweet Octoberfest!

Taffy apple & chips washed down with beer during the Superbowl.
I love mixing the sweet & salty.

Super crispy french fries atop a Chinese chicken salad, with mandarin oranges served by geisha belly dancer.

After building up an appetite (smoking a bowl with your homies), splurge on super well done scrambled eggs & bacon atop a cinnabon named Sandy (who is a belly dancer/dealer)

Meatball sandwich ala Elvis, with green peppers & melted swiss cheese & chips piled inside. Wolf down on top of Snookie from Jersey Shore. Then take turns shootin the meatballs off her beastly orangutan belly. She's living proof you can be short, ugly and obnoxious & get laid as long as your on TV.

Overpaid sitcom addict munchie: after bonging your brains out with five 19 yr.. old porn stars , pay them to get horizontal while you plotz on your middle aged ass and snort countless lines of chips ahoy off their nubile abs. Make sure your ex-wife and kids are in the connecting suite, so they can call 911 when you start trashing the room , tossing chocolate dipped hookers out the window.

Screaming kids at Applebees: pour appletini into his sippycup-
serve until kid shuts up! —Satisfies entire restaurant!

For a healthy snack: antipasta salad atop pepperoni pizza for sophisticated stoner prom queen.

Nachos and beer with Barbie Bachelorettes during Hot Tub search for studcicles. Bachelorettes should stew in a hot tub with 60 stanky HO's and an egomaniacal pig bachelor, making crème of chromosome soup.

Red velvet cupcakes with cream cheese frosting Popcorn, to gratify major munchies.

Corn-doggin' with your Hound Dog: Slide your corn dog inside a donut & dip in guacamole or cole slaw.

When you feel "Home Alone" because you're at an LA party of anorexic models, where there's no food, chow down on chicken & waffles in front of them , until they drop the crack pipe and join you.

Don't forget to feed the help! Party with your Chica! Share cheese & caramel corn with champagne chaser and play pin the tale on the sex-donkey to celebrate Cinco De Mayo!

QUICKIE RECIPES

GODDESS STUFFED SHROOMS

2 SLICES OF WHITE BREAD
(OR IF YOU HAVE TO BE HEALTHY, FAKE WHOLE WHEAT)
24 LARGE white MUSHROOMS
1 STICK OF BUTTER

TO SET THE MOOD, PLAY ONE OF MY VIDEOS: HOT BRA CONES, SPIKE IT, OR ONE OF MY ALBUMS, "BUY THIS AGAIN, PIGS"! THEN DRINK 1/2 GLASS OF WHITE WINE OR APPLE JUICE (IF YOU'RE IN AA), THEN" PREHEAT oven to 375. Cut stems from shrooms, Cut off dried icky stems and dispose. Dice the remaining good stems. Saute stems in butter for 3 minutes. Pretend you are "Mommie Dearest" and go mental & tear bread into very small pieces , then add to sautéed stems. (you may want to add sautéed celery, but don't stess about it. Ok, if you're adding sautéed celery, you might as well add shredded cheese. NowMix until bread is saturated, then stuff each mushroom cap with the stuffing mix. Bake on cookie sheet for about 20 minutes. Now go put some yogurt on your face & enjoy with gal pals.

HEY JUDE, HEY JUDE, I LOVE THOSE PEANUT BUTTER BARS!

I JAR of Peanut Butter ((16.3 oz.)I like crunchy, so just use it and SHUT UP!
1 1/2 cup powdered sugar
One 12 oz bag dark chocolate chips
3/4 stick of butter (don't cheap out with margarine, pigs)
11/2 cups graham cracker crumbs

Melt approx 2/3 jar of peanut butter & 3/4 stick of butter in microwave safe medium-large size bowl. Mix in 1/12 c each of graham cracker crumbs and powdered sugar. Mix it all up, then press into a pie tin. Melt a 12 oz bag of dark chocolate chips and por over top of mixture in pie tin. Place in your fridge for approx. 2 hours til set. Then sit our on counter (or on your lap) for another couple of hours to warm up (then it's easier to cut). Now cut and serve. not your hair, the Peanut butter bars, pigs!

BAKED SASSY SALMON

1 whole side of Salmon
Fresh Garlic to taste (approx 2 cloves-3 cloves)
petite amount of light butter

Cayenne Pepper
Seasoned Salt
Fresh Lemon

(This is for health nuts who need protein)
Place the whole side of salmon in aluminum foil. Spread with light butter. Add chopped fresh garlic. Sprinkle with cayenne pepper & seasoned salt. Seal and baked @ 350 for 30-45 minutes until fish flakes easily with fork. NOW WAKE UP FROM YOUR NAP, NARCOLEPTIC! Halfway through cooking, squeeze fresh lemon, then reseal & continue cooking. Then enjoy immediately, if you want to LIVE!

SASSY SPACE GODDESS COLESLAW

1 pkg. shredded coleslaw
1 cup chopped almonds
! cup chopped green onions
2 pkgs. of Ramen chicken flag noodles
(crumble & break apart)

2 spice packets from Ramen noodles
1/4 cup sugar
1/4 cup olive oil (extra virgin, slugs)
1/3 cup apple cider vinegar

Combine coleslaw, almonds, chopped green onions & crumbled noodles in a large bowl. Mix well. In a separate bowl combine the spice packets, sugar, olive oil, apple cider vinegar. Pour the dressing mixture over coleslaw and "set in fridge" not fried) for 2 hours before serving. Serve alone or as side dish with sassy salmon.

Most Fun in a Limo

The most fun I had in a limo was on the set of "Going Down In LA LA Land", John, "Michael" & the crew was about to shoot us getting out of the limo, & I said I want you to block my feet...he said why? I said because I'm wearing Betty White stockings, and they look nasty... and he said, "take them off".... I say, "John, I have to bend over like a Tijuana donkey dancer, right like I'm a stranger to that. So here I am on all fours & yell" Don't look at me!" Right like the gay boy is suddenly going to turn straight because I'm bent over like mike Tyson's butt boy in prison...hey, it could happen! Anyway I get the pantyhose half way down, & the DA opens the limo door and shouts "action & Michael & I are laughing hysterically, while screaming," no, we need a minute" and then w had to reshoot over and over until we stopped laughing.

Geishas

I need a wife- or a geisha following 2 ft.. behind me, picking up papers, socks, clearing the table, doing the dishes, the laundry, reorganizing the clothes in my closet.

Every girl should have a geisha boy- men want wives or maid/whores & women want butler/assistants- in short everyone wants a geisha-to pick up your dirty socks, laugh at your jokes and tell you who rocks, bow down and give you afternoon tea, and be invisible when necessary.

To scratch. Your back, prevent an attack, grease up your sacroiliac. Rub your toes, powder your nose, and wash out your nasty panty hose,

Fill you with gas, take out the trash, throw you a big fat birthday bash, and listen to you rant, dress you in hot pants, and flatter you like Cary Grant. dress you , be there to confess to, then bow & bless you. Get you a cold drink, make you think, make sure you pits don't stink. Catch you when you sink. Do my hair, apply the Nair, and give nosey Neighbors a scare.

Travels of The Goddess

If you ever travel through the south, please learn to speak "southern" if you want to live!! The first time I arrived in Nashville Tennessee, about 20 yrs....... ago, circa 1991, (that's pre Google, Twitter, sexting) I thought everyone would be a country singer or at least be a happy go lucky guitar player doing shots. Wrong!!! I hop into a cab from the airport, the driver, a grumpy curmudgeon, says, " strap yourself in, sister'. He immediately sensed I was a "Yankee bitch", and was not gonna let me forget it.

As we're driving, I tried to be friendly & said," where are the southern mansions?" he gripes" damn Yankees burned em

down!" I immediately slipped into my southern drawl, "I'm originally from Atlanta, and I hate those damn Yankees!

Everywhere I go, people are fascinated by the "mystique of Hollywood", and they think I am constantly rubbing elbows with the rich and famous. Wrong, everyone in la "acts" rich & famous. You soon realize every guy over

40 is a producer who has a three-picture deal while living in a shopping cart behind Starbucks.

I'm at a party this guy (who looks like a fat stoned Bruce Dern) is babbling about how he was a writer for the "Punky Brewster" and is now a "producer/ director, but has to hide his fame by being a handyman in the valley. Or else he would be swamped with fans. Right, Spielberg!

Bullying Is Not Restricted To Teens & Tweens

I get bullied in Trader Joe's parking lot =these soccer moms are bullies- one of em gave me the finger & bogarted right into the parking space my goddess-mobile was pulling into. , But I knew the green whore net would key my Mercedes & slash my tires and let's face it, $2 buck thorn whistle tofu tarts are just not worth it… so I pulled away and let the Whole Foods ho stick her nasty old Kia in the space!

I never had kids, in fact anytime I get melancholy about not having kids, I just look at my girlfriends whose teenagers scream at them "you won't even buy me a new car after I crashed your Camaro, how am I supposed to get to school…I hate you!!!! But if I did they would all be in "Toddlers & Tiaras" . There's nothing more appealing than a four yr.. old made up to look like a 20 yr.. old hooker singing, "man I feel like a woman" in Madonna bra cones.

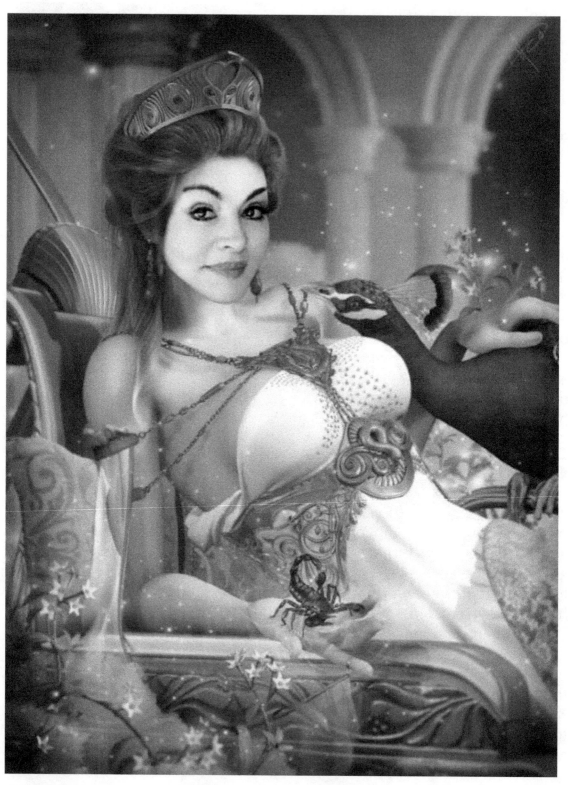

40 Ways to Breed A Love Slave

So many women ask, goddess after 10 years off the market due to that romance- killer called marriage, how do I prepare to date again? Ladies, and by ladies I include women in training (get it, west Hollywood, & san Fran-crisco). Again I say, ladies, in order to be totally prepared for dating, forget online dating, i.e. "it's just lies", like where they set you up on a blind lunch date, meaning you'll go blind upon meeting these trolls. I agreed to meet a lawyer at an upscale restaurant, "Applesleeze", he was so drunk, he tripped over the waiter, who's tray full of truffles flew into the face of a rodeo dr. Matron who's lips were so inflated she looked like marlin with a martini, I mean she had a serious case of Beverly Hills Housewife "trout pout". But getting back to husband hunting, all a man cares about is sleep food & sex & in that order. There is nothing that turns a guy on more than a nap after a big fat steak.

2. The way to a man's heart is through his love of sports & his stomach...- As men get older, all they want is spicy chicken wings & ESPN. Don't waste your time slaving over pot roast or rack of lamb...they want the rack of Dallas cowboy cheerleaders!

3. When making the decision to be intimate- do not, and I mean never come on like the slut that you are! Instead, use subtle sex talk such as: I'm a Goddess grenade and you are begging to pull my pin, soldier! And on the first night, don't whip out the Vietnamese love basket & your karma sutra moves because where do you go from there? Just lie there & tell him you're going to play a game? The Bolshevik revolution: you'll be Poland while he invades you !

4. Be a snob-bitch- that s right, carry yourself like Kim Kartrashian…(a few months ago I would have said Paris Hilton, but now she's about as popular as the Hilton hotels). So back to Kim, Every guy wants to saddle that bodacious billion dollar booty... why? Not just because she's a rich media-ho, but also because she let's you know upfront it is your life is mission to please her, or in 72 days you are replaceable…but she is not! That's the illusion you must create: you are irreplaceable. Oh yes, the pig may find a substitute, but he'll always hunger for you. It's like when you have a taste for a hot fudge sundae. You can't stop drooling about it, in fact you haven't eaten all day & that's what you crave. But you know it would blimp you out so instead you get a supersonic colonic… but that just makes you crave the forbidden hot fudge concoction even more, and you try to fight it with a wimpy Yoplait yogurt, fat free chips & salsa, so now you're gorging like an out of control pregnant woman and fill up on all this low-fat disgusting junk that ends up totaling more calories than the hot fudge sundae in the first place. So what's the lesson? Get what you really want in the first place or you'll pork yourself into fat pig anyway..

5. Go after what you want & then subtly grab it! I have observed many women in action. I know one in particular; let's call her Voracia- because her appetite for the very best was insatiable. She was vivacious, outgoing, and beautifully manipulative. Before the guy knew it, she had the deed to his house, and he didn't even tap her secret garden. It's like everyone wanted to please her. Homeless guys in front of Starbucks would give their mother's left kidney for a luscious latte look from her. Sounds like the queen of Sheba, right? Well almost... she was a greeter at Walmart! I ask you: who wouldn't want to worship that?

YOU'RE FIRED!

6. What are the qualities we're all looking for in a mate?

Yes we all want someone who is, thoughtful, reliable, generous, hot, fun and most importantly RIIIICH!! And not too good looking— like Ryan Gosling, because there will always be some slutcycle model who will throw herself at him & how many times can he turn that down? Also he can't be too rich like Donald trump because then you'll spend the whole day styling his comb over until you're forced to scream, "Donald, you're fired!!!!!

7. Never sleep with a guy on the first date, unless he's Hugh Jackman or Ryan Reynolds. A man has to be teased into pursuing you, no matter how horny you are for him, do not submit or you'll just be a notch on his belt. My friend, Trina was always bringing guys over to her place for an after dinner drink which turned into a make-out session on her chaise lounge- ladies, you must never do the chasing the pig must chase you!

8. Damsel in distress or slutty SOS: always ask a guy for help even if you can open the ketchup bottle, ask him- for 2 reasons: a. To insure he's not a wimp. And b. To make him feel like a man. In fact, the first time he stays at your place, loosen all of the light bulbs, so he can jump at the chance to screw them in.

After all as the goddess would say, how many men does it take to screw in a light bulb? All of them!!!

In fact, after you break up with the pig, the best way to pick up a new pig is to hang at home depot looking confused next to the screwdrivers. You'll either nail a plumber or a lesbian clerk to help you. If it's the lesbian, she'll build you a house & move in with you, and even if you break up with her, she'll stay and be your handyman while you're sleeping with your new squeeze in the den she just painted.

SGT. TENUTA

9. Pretend to be into his hobbies: basketball, monster truck rallies, jackrabbit breeding. Whatever it is, act totally fascinated till he puts that rock on your finger. I don't care if it's s watching dirt. If he's got money, tell him you adore dirt, and you'd love to travel the country in his Lamborghini observing it all: from the red clay in Georgia, to the snowcapped titons of Jackson Hole. If you have a problem with his lifestyle: watching sports, coin collecting, cross-dressing, don't scold him: join him- participate with your pig & you'll nail him. But do not go overboard and start dressing likes him or he'll drop you for a pole dancer from Poughkeepsie.

10. If a guy says he's not looking for a commitment…. He means it! But who cares? Your job is to get him to change his mind! Tie him up, tease him like crazy & then leave for a while. He'll knock down your door to be with you. And if that doesn't work, hunt him down. I had this girlfriend, bonnie, who became addicted to drugs, liquor and bad boys. Then she woke up at age 30 and she said to herself: I need to sober up and hook a great provider so I can be high: & at the same time have the finer things in life. She spotted a handsome, confirmed bachelor she couldn't live without, so did she flirt? No. Did she tease? No. She stalked him. I mean it: she told him on the first date: you're going to be the man I marry if it's the last thing I do! He just laughed, but within a month, she kicked his then girlfriend to the curb while she was recovering from a butt reduction, (yes…really). And then bonnie moved right in. In fact he confessed that her aggression turned him on so much that he made her his wife and secretary & for his booming extermination business.

Today, some 12 years later, they are worth over 30 million dollars & he knows if his eye wanders she'll drag his ass to court and make him pay through the nose. Needless to say, they are very happy…She tells him!

That leads me to the your number one goal in hooking the love hog:

Instill the fear of God in him: he has to know he will face your wrath if he cheats, or disrespects. You are the warden & he is your butt boy.

11. Live in the moment on the first few dates especially if he's a hottie. Oh, who am I kidding? If he's a hottie, you must daydream immediately about your nonexistent life together. As a potential Bridezilla, fast forward into the future while flirtatiously feeding him escargot, so you can fantasize about the names of your unborn children, your million dollar wedding, and of course your star-studded guest list including Lickme Blowhands and the Karcrashians!

12. You come first- but make him think it is he you want to please…and what better way to please him than to have your every whim met? He should call at least five times a day, but you only pick up once, and then he'll be so hungry for you, he'll drop his poker/bowling night with the boys just to take out the trash! Which by the way is a major turn on to all women. Men…if you want to score, you must take out the trash.. and lick us!

13. Listen to what his friends & family say about him. And then totally ignore them! Preferably he has no family or friends so you can totally possess him. If they say: oh he wants a home cooked meal and a few nights out with the boys… OK, tell him that he and his buddies can have a midlife crisis barbeque : all pile into a Porsche & down beer & bratwurst during Monday Night Football!

14. Spend equal time with your friends, do not drop them just because you're getting laid. Otherwise there's no challenge for your sex ape to capture your attention!!

15. Keep your options open for at least 3 days (okay weeks) before you decide to be exclusive + make him your oink blanket. Take it slowly, do not rush into the unknown, you need a minimum of 5 days to really know if this guy is even worthy to escort you to a nude midget mudwrestling cockfight!

16. Women of all ages say to me, "Goddess it's so hard to find a decent guy! To that the goddess says, "lower your standards damnit!!! Who do you think you are, so he has a hook hand and a Hoveround? Who cares, if he pays for valet? Just forget the tall handsome dream -stud- just fantasize about Brad Pitt & settle for a toad who can walk erect. Why? Because even toads have options: the internet has turned men into kids in a candy store if you don't put out, they'll just hop onto a heifer who will

17. Take control of his finances; that's right, you hold the MONEY!! Make it seem like you're doing him a favor to keep his banking records. Yep, it's called "occupy his wallet"! Give him an allowance with lots of Heineken so you can power shop at Nordstrom's.

18. Let him be the first to say the "L" word: and don't say it until you feel a diamond brewing in his pants! Men are carbon-based creatures for a reason to ultimately present us with giant engagement rings! He is not allowed to probe your petite princess canal with his one-eyed wonder worm until he gives you a diamond wrapped in a Bentley!

19. Only go on double dates w/ other couples if they are uglier than you! Then you don't have to worry about partner swapping unless you want it... then invite a hot looking couple, and play strip poker.

20. If you have kids, never and I mean never hire a cute nanny- the bitch should look like Jabba the Slut or your pig will cheat- you want examples? Christy Brinkley... how could any pig cheat on that hot supermodel? Robin Williams fell 4 his nanny & rumor has it that Brad Pitt stop is taking their nanny on horsey back rides while Lora Croft Tombraider is buying up orphans in Africa like Bridezilla at a Filene's basement wedding gown sale!

21. Never look for Mr. Right on Craig's-list- unless you want to end up at the Greyhound bus station stuffed in his suitcase.

22. Don't listen to Dr. Phil who says, "You don't need a guy to be whole & happy." Yes you do! Being single sucks the giant hippo!! - You need a guy / or mate to distract you from death- that's why everyone gets married- we don't want to be alone- you need someone to boss around and blame your bad decisions on!!!

23. Never point out your imperfections. Oh, my legs are too short- shut the hell up! Or at least you have some never say that within earshot of Heather Mills. Oh I have a third buttocks- great, J-Lo!!! All the brothers will worship at your feet. Your lust log should wake up every morning and say, "you are the most beautiful woman in the world"

24. Make sure he can be your best friend. He's the one you talk to first thing in the morning and the last one to tuck you in at night. Hot hate sex can only last so long; you need a companion who makes your life less stressful and more fun after fighting soccer moms for a parking space at Trader Joe's.

25. Never date or even spit in the direction of a troll who drives a "smart car" – these are not cars, they're organ donor dumpsters! And these are not men- they're morons who think driving in a sardine can is a harmless game of bumper cars.

26. No shacking up with your pig until he puts a ring on it or unless you need a green card to stay in the USA. But don't worry if you live in la, because LA is just Mexico with implants, so you cant be deported.

27. Never date a pig who is cheap, especially if after the 2nd date at taco hell, he says "I want to share everything with you", then hands you the tab. Kick the pig to the curb. I let my ex-crement live in my house for 10 years, rent-free, and we'd go to Shakey's pizza & he'd ask, would you like me to get this? Oh… could you spare it, madeoff?

28. A relationship needs stability. Breakup make up sex is great, but if there are constant ups and downs, it's not a romance, it's a ride at Six Flags and you're just going to hurl chunks once you get off!!!

29. Don't ever start cooking for him… unless you're already fat and he is a chubby-chaser. Once you start cooking, you eat your weight in pasta, pizza & pastries & expand into a steakasaur-ass. Make the pig take you out to nice restaurants, so you can blimp out together. Then you'll be too fat to leave each other!

30. Workout together. Every morning do yoga in bed. Play some Enya & stretch until you intertwine into a human pretzel!!

Never date a guy whose thighs are thinner than yours!! My friend Shasta had redwood thighs, every time she walked, they'd rub together & start a fire. If that's your problem, you need to pump your pig with steroids

31. Never date a married man-pig

If he's married and dating, obviously, he's not just dating you, sugar pants! So wake up and smell the pollinating pig's perfume! Notice he's never around on holidays; cuz one of his "kids" needs him? And don't give me this lame excuse that you didn't have a clue he was hitched…hello. He never sleeps over, you're not allowed at his house, in fact, you don't even know where he lives! When he does treat you to dinner at "the olive garden", his cell phone constantly rings and he says" I have to take this". Then he skedaddles like the roadrunner, and you're stuck with the bill. He's missing in action for a week, no calls, no texts. Then as fate would have it, a week later you run into him at "Forever 21" where he's hitting on mall chicks who are oohing and aaaing over his 2 yr old twins while wifey is getting a manly-pedi.

So I repeat, Never date a guy who has a girlfriend/wife why? Because he's taken!!! Even if he's in process of getting divorced. Tell him to take care of his unfinished business and then he can focus on you!!!

32. Don't complement him too much, especially if he's hot...do the yoko-act like you're unimpressed, then he'll work to win you over. Men need a quest. Like Don Quixote, fighting windmills & wizards like Charlie Sheen.

33. If he's a hot bad boy, grab him, even if it only lasts a few months. All women need a hot Viking to get their juices flowing.

34. Mick Jagger said in a movie " I spent my whole life trying to please women, now I just want to please one." Liar- men spend their lives feeding women a load of crap to transform them into horizontal sperm receptacles. The only reason they finally settle down with one woman is not because you are the one…. Its' because they are fucking tired, and you're the one they landed on!

35. Men do not take hints…you have to hit them over the head with a hundred pound weight to get what you want! For example, my birthday was coming up, and being the delicate flower I am, I had my girlfriends hint to my boyfriend, that I would like a flat screen TV. He said, I don't get appliances for my significant other until we've been together for 10 years. To which they replied, "you've been dating for 5 months…in LA that is 10 years. So he gave me a flat screen TV!

36. Keep your fights fair & the sex sassy!!!! Unless you really want to delete your love donkey, no verbal jabs below the belt! Never insult his manhood. If he has a problem with take-off, don't berate him, just whip out your pocket rocket and watch BrokeBack Mountain.

37. Do not nag. If he's on his computer more than he is on you…he's into porn…so have porn night….Wear your sexy, feathery nothings, pop the corn, watch "Debbie Does Dallas" and if he's still addicted to his mac…..Next!

38. Let the guy go to his cave to pout. Of course his cave should preferably be at the designer section of sex 5th avenue, so that when he snaps out of his funk, he will have the good sense to buy you a louis vuitton bag. Men do not want to talk, they don't want to hear about your day,they just want to grunt and hunt!

39. Do not date a doctor unless you want to be kept waiting for 50 minutes while he's giving a "rectal" to his head nurse, only to quickly feel you up, so he can probe his next temp-tart.

40. Only date a stud who orders what you want, and then lets you eat off of his plate. It's called sharing. My ex would slap my petite paws when I would reach for a French fry, so ofcourse I banned him from the Temple of Judyism!"

The First Lady definitely eats off the President's plate. He's manorexic, while she's got a back porch that you can play ping pong on! And I mean it as a compliment. Hey Michele, Barack is the new "Terminator" who took down BinLaden, Ghadafi, and George W, so 86 the asparagus, and treat him to a double cheeseburger stuffed with french fries and a chocolate shake! Yum!

CPSIA information can be obtained
at www.ICGtesting.com
Printed in the USA
LVHW050826110123
736853LV00013B/852